VENUS IN THE KITCHEN:
RECIPES FOR SEDUCTION

by Pilaff Bey
Edited by Norman Douglas

 FTER all these years it is a moving experience to see the name of Norman Douglas upon a new book. True, he claims to have done no more than edit this collection of culinary recipes, compiled, he says, by a friend whom the reader will strongly suspect to be mythical.

♥ The author explains that "after a succulent dinner with several bottles of red wine", some of the elder guests began to lament their declining vigor. Someone suggested that there must be certain dishes whose ingredients and spices would be likely to revive the fading ardours of middle age. The author then began to make a collection of these recipes.

♥ The reader must be left to prove their aphrodisiacal value by personal experiment. But whatever their success in this respect, it will be granted that neither Marcel Boulestin nor Escoffier himself would be likely to find fault with his fillets of sole à la Pompadour, rolled around truffles and mushrooms and cooked in white wine, nor many another dish which could be cooked and enjoyed in civilized homes even now, quite apart from their value as aphrodisiacs. But oysters have long been known to be efficacious in this respect, and for them there are many recipes: boiled oysters, oyster olive, oysters in champagne and wine are some of them.

♥ Not every gourmet can obtain *skink,* which is an aphrodisiacal reptile only to be found in the deserts of Africa or Arabia; nor will he be able to "clean and truss a young crane", or obtain a sufficiency of leopard's marrow to cook in goat's milk (this for timid persons).

♥ There is also a section of aphrodisiacal drinks, including a tonic wine for aged persons, and a recuperative drink containing maraschino, brandy, cream and an egg. This latter will be very necessary if some of the other recipes fulfill their purpose. Anyway, the book will be an abiding delight to every cultured eye, whatever its aphrodisiacal success may be.

VENUS IN THE KITCHEN:
RECIPES FOR SEDUCTION

"En cuisine surtout, rien ne s'obtient de rien."
—BARON DE BRISSE

VENUS IN THE KITCHEN

Painting by D. H. Lawrence

VENUS IN THE KITCHEN:
RECIPES FOR SEDUCTION

By Pilaff Bey
Edited by Norman Douglas
Introduction by Graham Greene

HALO BOOKS
San Francisco

Library of Congress Cataloging-in-Publication Data

Bey, Pilaff, 1868-1952.
    Venus in the Kitchen: Recipes for Seduction / by Pilaff Bey; edited by
Norman Douglas; with an introduction by Graham Greene.

    p.   cm.

    Includes index.
    ISBN 1-879904-01-2 : $13.95
    1. Cookery.   I. Douglas, Norman, 1868-1952.   II. Title.
    TX652.B4974   1992
    641.5—dc20

                        91-28238
                         CIP

First published 1952, Kingswood, Surrey, England.

© Halo Books, San Francisco, 1992

Printed by Griffin Printing
Typography by BookPrep

HALO BOOKS
P.O. Box 2529 ● San Francisco, CA 94126

Cover and interior design by Susan Larson

TO

THE MEMORY OF

EMILIO

CONTENTS

Illustrations

INTRODUCTION

N those last years you would always find him between six and dinner-time in the Café Vittoria, unfashionably tucked away behind the Piazza. Through the shabby windows one stared across at Naples—one could go only a few steps further without tumbling off the island altogether. Crouched over an aperitif (too often in the last years almost unalcoholic), his fingers knotted with rheumatism, squawking his "Georgio, Georgio" to summon the devoted waiter who could hear that voice immediately above all the noises of Capri, snow-white hair stained here and there a kind of butterfly-yellow with nicotine, Douglas sat on the borders of the kingdom he had built house by house, character by character, legend by legend.

♥ One remembers him a few months before he died, handling the typescript of this book, re-sorting the loose carbon pages: there wasn't enough room on the café table what with the drinks, the old blue beret, the snuff-box, the fair copy; the wind would keep on picking up a flimsy carbon leaf and shifting it out of place, but the old ruler was back at the old game of ruling. He wouldn't have given even the menial task of assembly to another. With a certain fuss of pleasure and a great tacit pride he was handling a new book of his own again. There hadn't been a new book for—how many years? Sometimes something seemed to be wrong with the type-script: a monologue of exaggerated grumbles marked the misprints—not one of those earlier misprints carefully pre-served in proof, to be corrected later in manuscript gratis for a friend and at a price for collectors—"Cost him a tenner, my dear"—and that sudden laugh would break like an explosion in a quarry, over before the noise has reached you.

♥ My generation was brought up on *South Wind*, although I suppose the book was already five years old before we opened it and read the first sentence, "The bishop was feeling rather sea-sick," which seemed to liberate us from all the serious dreary immediate past. Count Caloveglia, Don Francesco, Cornelius van Koppen, Miss Wilberforce, Mme. Steynlin, Mr. Eames, Saint Dodekanus, the Alpha and Omega Club: Nepenthe had not been Capri, but Capri over half a century has striven with an occasional success to be Nepenthe. *South Wind* appeared in 1917, superbly aloof from the catastrophes of the time: it was the age of Galsworthy, Wells, Bennett, Conrad: of a sometimes inflated, of a sometimes rough-and-ready prose. Novelists were dealing with "big" subjects—family panoramas, conflicts of loyalty. How reluctantly we came to the last sentence: "For it was obvious to the meanest intelligence that Mr. Keith was considerably drunk." This wasn't the world of Lord Jim of the Forsytes or the dreary Old Wives.

♥ *South Wind* was to have many inferior successors: a whole Capri school. Douglas was able to convey to others some of his tolerance for human foibles: characters like Mr. Parker and Mr. Keith were taken up like popular children and spoiled. It became rather easy to write a novel, as the reviewers would say, "in the manner of *South Wind*." None of Douglas's disciples had learnt to write as he had. Nearly a quarter of a century of clean, scholarly, exact writing, beginning so unrewardingly with a Foreign Office report on the Pumice Stone Industry of the Lipari Islands by the Third Secretary of Her Majesty's Embassy in St. Petersburg, published by the Stationery Office at the halfpenny, went to the creation of Perelli's Antiquities and "the unpublished chronicle of Father Capocchio, a Dominican friar of licorous and even licentious disposition, a hater of Nepenthe. . . "

♥ Douglas died in the middle eighties after a life consistently open, tolerant, unashamed. "Ill spent" it has been called by the kind of judges whose condemnation is the highest form of praise. In a sense he had created Capri: there have been suicides, embezzlements, rapes, thefts, funerals and processions which we feel would not have happened exactly in that way if Douglas had not existed, and some of his tolerance perhaps touched even the authorities when they came to deal with those events.

♥ It is fitting, I think, that his last book should be as unserious and shameless as this collection of aphrodisiac recipes, to close a life in which he had enjoyed varied forms of love, left a dozen or so living tokens here and there, and been more loved himself than most men. (One remembers the old gypsy family from northern Italy who travelled all the way to Capri to spend an afternoon with Douglas and proudly exhibit to him another grandchild.) With its air of scholarship, its blend of the practical—the almond soup—and the wildly impracticable—Rôti sans Pareil, the crispness of the comments (we only have to add his customary endearments to hear the ghost speak): "Very stimulating, my dear," "Much ado about nothing," "Not very useful for people of cold temperament," with a certain dry mercilessness in the introduction, this book will be one of my favourite Douglases: it joins *Old Calabria, Fountains in the Sand, They Went, Looking Back, London Street Games*, the forbidden anthology of limericks.

♥ He will be delighted in the shades at any success we may have with his recipes and bark with laughter at our ignominious failures, and how pleased he will be at any annotations and additions, so long as they are exact, scholarly, uninflated, and do not carpingly arise from a cold temperament. For even his enormous tolerance had certain limits. He loved life too well to have much patience with puritans or fanatics. He was a gentleman and he disliked a boor. One of the finest passages of invective written in our time is his pamphlet against D. H. Lawrence in defence of Maurice Magnus, and an echo of that old controversy can be found in these pages.

"Not many years ago I met in the South of France a Mr. D. H. Lawrence, an English painter, whom I interested in this subject and who certainly looked as if his own health would have been improved by a course of such recipes as I had gathered together."

♥ There are said to be certain Jewish rabbis who perform the operation of circumcision with their thumbnail so rapidly and painlessly that the child never cries. So without warning Douglas operates and the victim has no time to realise in what purgatorio of lopped limbs he is about to awake, among the miserly, the bogus, the boring and the ungenerous.

GRAHAM GREENE

PREFACE

HE following recipes were collected not in a hurry, nor with the intention of publishing them. They were collected slowly, one by one, for the private use and benefit of a small group of friends, most of whom, I am sorry to say, are older than they want to be, and all of them anxious—who is not?—to preserve for as long as may be possible the vitality of their youth and middle age.

♥ I began one night twelve years ago after we had enjoyed a succulent dinner with several bottles of old red wine, followed by bitter lamentations on the part of the older members of the party over their declining vigour, in the course of which one of them remarked: "Something might be done in the way of culinary recipes," adding that a well-known authority, Liebault, had written upon the rejuvenating effects of certain condiments and certain dishes. I was then and there deputed, or rather implored, to look into the subject and to note down such recipes as might apply to their case. This I did, supplying them with copies.

♥ Twelve years is a long period of time, and no doubt I could have made a larger selection in the interval, but my leisure is not wholly given up to researches of this kind, important as they may be to persons of mature age. I have other "hobbies", as they are called, such as the collecting of Persian carpets and the writing of a book, begun in 1902, on the varieties of Central Asian melons, which are the finest in the world— whatever certain American friends may say to the contrary (I have been to their country; they have not been to Khiva).

♥ Not many years ago I met in the South of France a Mr. D. H. Lawrence, an English painter, whom I interested in this subject and who certainly looked as if his own health could have been improved by a course of such recipes as I had gathered together. He became so enthusiastic that he drew for me the frontispiece which adorns this book. I reproduce it because I understand that many of his admirers will be glad to see a new example of his art. For my own part, I must confess that this picture of a fat naked woman pushing a loaf into an oven is not at all my notion of *Venus in the Kitchen*. I think such a creature would scare a good many people out of the kitchen, and perhaps out of the house.

♥ In spite of that artistic encouragement I kept the recipes at the bottom of my trunk, adding a fresh one every now and then and also an occasional freak-dish of an aphrodisiacal nature. There they would have stayed but for a member of that group of friends whom I have mentioned, and who lived at Smyrna before the Turkish occupation and has since died. He tried one or two of them, and was favourably impressed by their subsequent effects. They worked, he said. He begged me to have them printed, and said that in so doing I might confer a benefit on some poor devil. The poor devil, he explained, must be a rich one, else he had better abandon all hope of encountering Venus, and retain that frigidity of temperament for which the economical recipes of ordinary cookery books are responsible. Well, I hope the poor devil, whoever he is, will follow his example and achieve the same happy results.

Pilaff Bey

♥ P.S.—The foregoing pages and all that follows were written not later than 1936.

♥ From the original collection I have expunged some fifty recipes, notably those of sweet dishes in whose aphrodisiac virtues I have no great faith, while retaining a few delectable absurdities to show the length to which humanity will go in its search for the lost vigour of youth.

♥ And let me once more thank Faith Compton Mackenzie for her choice contributions, as well as Sybille Bedford, without whose friendly help and expert knowledge of matters culinary many mistakes might have crept into the text.

P. B.

June, 1951.

SOUPS

ALMOND SOUP

LANCH a quart of almonds and pound them in the mortar with the yolks of six hard-boiled eggs till they come to a fine paste. Mix them by degrees with a quart of chicken stock, and a quart of cream. Stir well together, and when well mixed, put in a saucepan over a gentle fire, and keep stirring all the time. Take care it does not curdle. Serve when hot.

BROAD BEAN SOUP

OOK the broad beans in salted water with a ham bone. Add a pinch of chopped parsley and a pinch of saffron. When the beans are well cooked, pass through a sieve, leaving some whole ones behind which you will add to the soup later. Put the liquid again on the fire and when boiling add a handful of rice and the few beans left over. When the rice is cooked, serve with grated Parmesan cheese. Highly recommended.

CELERY CREAM

EAL the celery, cut in small pieces, scald it, and drain in a colander.

Now put it in a saucepan over the fire with a piece of butter; sprinkle it with a pinch of flour; moisten it with some good thickened stock; bind it with the yolk of eggs mixed with cream, flavour it with a little nutmeg and serve hot.

CRAYFISH SOUP

TAKE about fifty large fresh-water crayfish; wash them repeatedly, changing the water every time, and leave them to drain. Then put them to cook in a saucepan with some good stock, a carrot and some parsley.

When they are cooked, remove the saucepan from the fire and leave it open for seven or eight minutes; then take out the shell-fish and throw them in a strainer or colander, and keep the broth.

When the prawns are half cold, peel them, and put the shells and heads in a mortar. Pound them to a purée.

Soak a lump of soft bread in the broth in which the prawns have been boiled; dry the softened bread by putting it in the oven, and then put it in the mortar to work it in with the purée.

Add the broth and thin the mixture, if necessary, with stock; pass it through a sieve into a saucepan, which should be put back on the fire, adding the prawns; stir, and do not allow it to boil. Salt to taste, add a little Cayenne pepper, and serve.

An approved aphrodisiac.

CONSOMMÉ VIVEUR

AKE some good strong consommé and bring it to a lively boil. Throw in a handful or two of fresh celery, stalks, leaves and all, and cook, uncovered, for about five minutes.

Fish out the celery, cloud the consummé with a teaspoonful of cream and serve at once, sprinkled with a little chopped chervil.

Very stimulating indeed.

EEL SOUP

AKE a big eel, clean and wash it two or three times in water, and then once in vinegar. Put it to boil in a saucepan together with two onions scorched on the fire, one or two bay-leaves, a sliced carrot, a few pieces of celery and fennel, pepper and salt. Boil for about two hours, then rub liquid and all through a sieve, seeing that the flesh of the fish passes well through. Put it on the fire, adding a piece of butter and a spoonful of tomato sauce. Serve hot with small pieces of toast.

EASTER RICE

OR three persons place on the fire a pot with four or five pints of chicken broth; when boiling put in a small handful of rice for each person and let it cook. Meanwhile prepare in your soup tureen three spoonfuls of grated Parmesan cheese, a little grated nutmeg, and three yolks of egg; mix together. When the rice is cooked, pour, little by little, rice and broth over the mixture, stirring continually and seeing that the egg does not curdle.

FENNEL SOUP

AKE three or four big fennels, and remove the outer parts. Put them in fresh water for at least two hours. Have some thin stock ready on the boil; season with salt. Cut your fennels and put them into the stock. When well cooked, pass through a sieve. Put the liquor in the saucepan again, add a cupful of cream and bring it up to the boil. Serve it with fried croûtons.

HARE SOUP

AKE the legs and head of a hare and put it to boil in four or five quarts of water with a ham bone, one big onion (which you have roasted before on the fire), two or three pieces of celery, one clove of garlic, a *bouquet garni* composed of a small sprig of rosemary, basil, thyme, marjoram, a stick of cinnamon, about ten cloves, twenty peppercorns, and a pinch of saffron. Boil till the meat is practically cooked into rags. Take the flesh of the hare, throwing away the bones, and pound it into a paste, pass it through a sieve and mix it with the liquor. Put on the fire and thicken by stirring in a paste made of the raw liver of the hare pounded with a little cream and a dash of good brandy.

Do not allow to boil, but serve very hot with croûtons.

PRAWN OR SHRIMP SOUP À LA CERTOSINA

THIS is prepared in the same way as the fresh-water crayfish (page 6), a variety of *potage bisque.*

You need extra prawns and some force-meat balls of fish for a garnish.

Pour your soup into a tureen which already con-tains yolks of egg thickened with 100 grammes of butter and a glass of Madeira.

The whole should be served at table as soon as ready and very hot.

Try it!

PURÉE OF CELERY

 AKE a bunch of celery and wash it well; cut it in pieces and place it in a saucepan with water and a little salt. Boil throughly, drain, and put in cold water.

In another saucepan melt over the fire an ounce of butter, one ounce of flour, salt, pepper and a pinch of grated nutmeg; mix all together, adding the celery, a quart of broth, and the same amount of cream. Put it on the fire, taking care to stir until it boils, press through a sieve and again put it on the fire for a moment.

Rather banal, I venture to think.

PURÉE OF FOWL À LA REINE

LEAN a chicken, and put it in a saucepan with a quart of broth, a carrot, an onion, and three or four cloves. Simmer very gently for three hours; take out the fowl, cut off the white meat, and pound very fine. Remove the grease carefully from your soup in which the fowl has been cooked, then add the pounded chicken, and put through a sieve. Heat it up again on the fire, add a pint and a half of cream, taking care that it does not boil, add a little nutmeg, pepper, salt, an ounce of butter, and the yolks of four eggs.

A French classical recipe.

PURÉE OF GAME

UT on the fire in an earthenware pot a partridge, a hare, and a neck of veal in an excellent beef stock; skim it and then add carrots, onions and celery. When the game is cooked take it out of the pot, remove the bones, let it half cool and pound in a mortar. Add some crumbs of bread soaked in the gravy and pound it again; mix everything thoroughly and pass it through a sieve. The purée thus obtained should be thinned with gravy passed through a strainer; then heat it up again without letting it come to the boil. Serve with croûtons.

Americans of a certain age, if they cared more for game than they do, might learn to appreciate the mildly stimulating effects of this purée.

STURGEON SOUP
À LA CHINOISE

ROCURE the head of a large sturgeon, saw it in halves from the back of the head down to the snout; then saw the halves into pieces the size of your fist, and place them in a large-sized pan with cold water to soak for several hours; taking care to wash them and change the water frequently.

Next, put the pieces of sturgeon into a large stew-pan in plenty of cold water, and set them on the fire to boil gently until the husk or shell is easily detached from the pieces of cartilage or gristle; place the latter, when thoroughly freed from the meaty and fatty substance, in a large stewpan; moisten with good veal stock in sufficient quantity to make soup enough for the number of guests. Garnish with carrots, onions, celery, a faggot of parsley, green onions, marjoram, thyme, and sweet basil, three blades of mace, twelve cloves, and twenty pepper-corns; boil gently for about two hours.

As soon as you find that the pieces of cartilage are transparent and rather soft to the touch, they must be immediately drained upon a sieve, and the liquor placed in a clean stewpan and set beside a stove-fire, adding half a bottle of good sherry and a small pinch of Cayenne. Allow the soup to boil gently by the side of the stove for about half an hour, taking care to remove all the scum and grease that rises to the surface; after which add the pieces of cartilage and the juice of a lemon, and serve.

This soup is very strengthening; the wine, lemon juice, and Cayenne may be dispensed with for invalids. The head of the sturgeon forms an excellent substitute for turtle, and may be dressed after the same manner.

(From C. E. Francatelli: *The Modern Cook.*)

RICE

BLACK RISOTTO

LEAN well half a pound of cuttlefish, keeping apart the little bag containing the ink. Cut the fish into small pieces and leave them in fresh water for half an hour.

Chop fine a big onion, two cloves of garlic, half a red pimento; add pepper and salt. Put these in a saucepan with three spoonfuls of fine olive oil. Fry. When the onion is getting brown, throw in the fish and let it cook till it gets yellow. Then add half a pound of chopped spinach and let it cook for thirty minutes. Add then a pound of rice and the little bags from the fish which contain the ink, mix well with a wooden spoon in order to break the bags and pour in little by little some hot water with diluted tomato sauce in it. When the rice is cooked, add a piece of butter and some Parmesan cheese. The rice must absorb all the liquid and be nearly dry, if you want to have a good *risotto nero*.

PILAFF OF MUTTON

AVE about a pound and a half of neck of mutton boiled, putting to boil with it one onion, a branch of celery, one carrot and a bay-leaf, pepper and salt.

Heat a quarter of a pound of butter in a stewpan and dry in it one ounce of blanched and shredded almonds together with a chopped onion and a dessert-spoonful of stoned raisins. When these are brown, strain them from the butter and place them aside. Heat the butter up again, put in half a pound of rice and fry it a very light brown. Strain off the butter and add little by little the stock in which the mutton has been boiled after having strained it and taken off the fat. Stir continually and add pepper, salt, two cloves, a pinch of cayenne and one of cinnamon. Now cut your mutton into small pieces, make a well in the centre of the rice, lay in the mutton pieces, heap the rice on them and cook all together for about thirty minutes. To serve, place the mutton pieces in a heap in the centre of a dish and the rice round, and garnish with the fried raisins, almonds and onions.

RICE WITH SHRIMPS

HOP very fine a branch of celery, a small carrot, half an onion, a clove of garlic, and put all in a pan with a small piece of butter and half a spoonful of olive oil and fry till brown. Have ready half a pound of shelled shrimps. Take half of them and let them fry with the above ingredients for a few minutes, season with pepper and salt, and go on adding hot water little by little till you have put enough for cooking in it one pound of rice. Let the water boil at least a quarter of an hour.

Pass through a sieve, seeing that the meat of the shrimps goes well through. When passed, put it in a saucepan over the fire, and when boiling add one pound of rice and a piece of butter. Let the rice absorb the liquid. If it becomes too dry before being cooked, add a little hot water, but the rice must not be too moist. When nearly cooked, add the other half of the shrimps, mix well, and serve with grated Parmesan cheese.

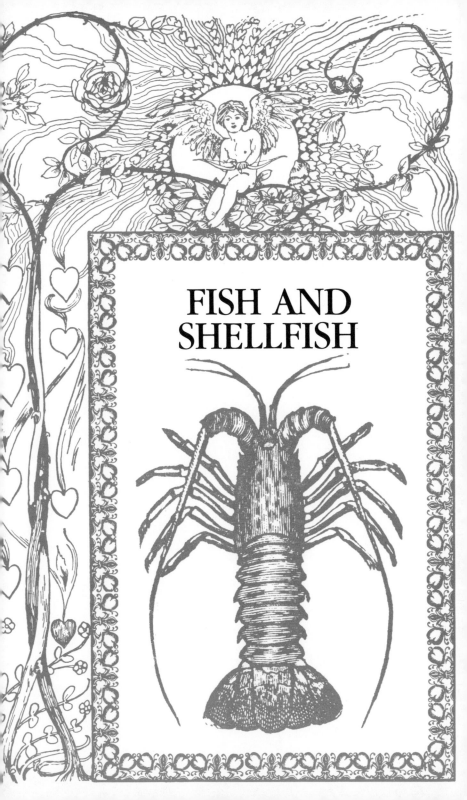

FISH AND
SHELLFISH

ATHENIAN EELS

AKE some good stock, a few mushrooms, one tablespoonful of vinegar, one of French mustard, one of anchovy sauce, and a little chopped parsley. Mix all the above together in a stewpan and let it simmer for about fifteen minutes.

Have your eels cut into small pieces, after having them washed and dried with a cloth. Flour them lightly and put them to fry in boiling olive oil. When fried put them on a dish and pour over them the above sauce. Serve very hot.

BAKED EELS

OR three pounds of eels put in a casserole four ounces of butter, set it on a good fire, and when melted sprinkle in it a teaspoonful of flour, stirring the while; also, a pinch of grated nutmeg, salt, pepper, saltspoonful of chopped parsley, two or three mushrooms, also chopped, then the eels. Pour on it a glass of white wine, and a liqueur-glass of French brandy; cover the casserole, take it from the fire, and put it in a moderately heated oven, and serve when done just as it is, in the casserole.

Nothing can be better—for those who like eels.

CACCIUCCO

 LIVORNESE dish which corresponds to the French Bouillabaisse.

Usually the following fish is used: a small eel, small red mullets, mussels, mackerel, pieces of big fish stock such as sturgeon, dog-fish or others. Take about two pounds of these fish, a quarter of a pound of fresh tomatoes, one onion, two cloves of garlic, two spoonfuls of olive oil, two spoonfuls of vinegar, a sprig of thyme, half a dry red pimento, some parsley, salt and pepper.

Chop fine the onion, parsley, thyme, garlic and pimento. Put them into a saucepan with the oil and fry till the onion gets brown, then add the tomatoes already cut into small pieces, season with pepper and salt and let the tomato cook well. Add then vinegar and a little water if necessary. Boil for five minutes and strain the liquid. Put it on the fire again together with the fish. When the fish is cooked, add half a spoonful of oil. Have some toasted bread ready at the bottom of a soup tureen and pour over it the fish and liquor.

Serve hot.

CRAYFISH À LA SYBARITE

FRY lightly in butter two onions and three carrots already sliced finely, with chopped parsley and thyme. Throw in the crayfish, which you must have already cut into pieces. Cook the pieces on both sides, then add some spice as: a small pinch of cinnamon, a little grated nutmeg, and a pinch or two of paprika. Add a spoonful of butter, and when this is melted, throw in half a bottle of dry champagne, which must never boil. Cook for half an hour and serve hot.

EELS À LA DEL SBUGO

A BIG eel is necessary, from which you remove the inside. Wash well and skin, leaving the head attached to the skin. Put the skin in vinegar and water, and leave it there till you have done the next operation.

Boil the flesh of the eel in water together with a slice of lemon, a piece of celery, a small carrot, and a few cloves. When you see that it can be detached from the bone, take it out from the water, let it cool and then bone it, being careful not to break the bone, which you put aside.

Now pulp the flesh in a mortar, together with a few blanched almonds, a spoonful of sultana raisins, a pinch of sugar, one of cinnamon, and some finely chopped aromatic herbs, pepper and salt.

Take the skin out of the infusion, dry it well, and put it first on a board. Make a layer of the pulp inside it, place in the middle the bone and cover it with the rest of the pulp. Roll it up and stitch it, seeing that it gets the same form of the eel as before.

Brush it with olive oil all over, place it on a baking dish, and cook it in a hot oven till the skin is crisp.

Serve hot after having sprinkled with sugar and cinnamon.

FILLETS OF SOLE

AKE some fillets of sole, flour them, fry them in butter in a saucepan, add two glasses of champagne, sliced truffles, some mushrooms, some cream, and a good pinch of Hungarian paprika. Let the fillets simmer for about fifteen minutes. Sprinkle over with chopped parsley. Serve hot.

FILLETS OF SOLE
À LA POMPADOUR

ILLET the soles, and after having covered them with a mixture of truffles and mushrooms finely chopped, roll them up and cook them in white wine, adding a bunch of aromatic herbs and salting to taste.

Strain the sauce, add some fish stock, and thicken with two yolks of egg.

Put the fillets on a dish, arranged round a centre of peeled prawns, pour the sauce over, and serve hot.

FROGS' LEGS

UT three dozen frogs' legs in a saucepan with a dozen chopped mushrooms, four shallots also chopped, and two ounces of butter. Toss them on a fire for five minutes; then add a tablespoon of flour, a little salt and pepper, grated nutmeg; and moisten with a glass of white wine and a teacupful of consommé.

Boil for ten minutes, meanwhile mix the yolks of four eggs with two tablespoonfuls of cream. Now remove the frogs' legs and the other ingredients from the fire, then add the eggs and cream, stirring continually until thoroughly mixed, and serve.

A noble aphrodisiac.

LANGOUSTE
À L'AMERICAINE

HE best recipe for this dish is given by Charles Monselet.

Take a superb and lively crayfish, cut it in pieces, and throw it, still breathing, into finest oil in a saucepan on a very hot fire, add salt, pepper, a little chopped garlic, some good white wine, good sauce of fresh tomatoes, plenty of spices. Cook for about half an hour; put in at the last minute a little *demi-glacé* stock, and dust lightly with Cayenne pepper.

Monselet declares that if the chaste Joseph had been given this dish by Potiphar's wife, she would not have been snubbed on that memorable occasion.

POTTED LOBSTER

AKE the meat of the lobster, cut it in slices and put it in a stewpan with a piece of butter. Add to a pound of lobster four boned anchovies and some peppercorns, a pinch of salt; let the lobster simmer gently over the fire for twenty minutes. Now pound it in a mortar and pass through a sieve. Put it in a small pot, press it well down, and let it get cold. Then serve it.

RED MULLETS IN SHRIMP SAUCE

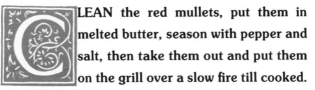

CLEAN the red mullets, put them in melted butter, season with pepper and salt, then take them out and put them on the grill over a slow fire till cooked.

Have ready the following gramolade: Take some olive oil, add chopped parsley, a spoonful of capers, a finely chopped spring onion. Pound well several shrimps and add them to the above, with the juice of a lemon and a little French mustard. Mix thoroughly, work it well, and serve hot with the grilled mullets.

SCALLOPED CRAB

 OIL the crab for eight or ten minutes; when cold take out of the shell all the part good to eat and chop it. Mix it then with a beaten egg, have it seasoned with red pepper and salt. Make apart a béchamel with milk, butter, and white flour. When the béchamel is made, take it away from the fire and add to it three spoonfuls of grated Parmesan of Gruyère, and yolks of two eggs. Mix now the crab together with the béchamel. Have your shells slightly buttered and fill them in with the mixture. Put them in a hot oven, and when you see they begin to get a golden colour on the top, serve them hot.

Not very invigorating.

SCAVECCILAFF

UT into pieces two good-sized eels, after having washed them in water, and then in vinegar.

Put a spoonful of olive oil into a frying-pan, and when boiling fry the pieces of eel in it till they become crisp. Take them out and drain well.

Now put in a saucepan two glasses of vinegar with chopped onion, half a chilli, a spray of rosemary, a crushed clove of garlic, a few cloves, two bay-leaves, and three hard-boiled yolks of egg cut into pieces.

Boil for at least twenty minutes, and then pass through a sieve.

Place your pieces of eel in a deep dish and pour the above liquor over them.

Serve cold the day after.

SKINK

(a reptile aphrodisiac)

HE skink is lauded as a stimulant by many ancients.

The difficulty will be to find it. But if someone chances to be in Africa or Arabia he will be able to do so. One way of cooking skink is the following:

Fillet them (along the backbone), soak them in beaten eggs, season, and fry in olive oil. Mesue preferred the tails of skink. Tristram speaks well of roasted skink.

Arabs still make use of it; the ancient Greeks did likewise, and Pliny the Elder has left us a Roman recipe which differs from the one here given.

STEWED CRABS

OIL a dozen fine large crabs about five minutes in order to kill them. Take them off the fire and when sufficiently cooled cut off the claws and crack, separating the joints. Remove the "apron" or *tablier* of the crab and the "dead man's fingers", and take off the spongy substance. These are the portions that are uneatable. Remove the shell, cut the body of the crab into four parts, cutting down the centre across.

Chop a large onion very fine and brown with butter or lard, using a tablespoonful of either. Add a dozen large fresh tomatoes, chopped fine, in their liquor, and brown nicely; stir in chopped celery, thyme, parsley, one bay-leaf chopped fine; pepper and salt to taste, and a dash of Cayenne pepper. Add one clove of garlic, chopped fine. Taste and add more seasoning if necessary. Let the mixture cook ten minutes, then add the crabs and let them cook ten minutes longer.

Crab is recommended as an aphrodisiac by several poets (and so, by the way, are crab apples).

STURGEON IN ANCHOVY SAUCE

LEAN and open a small sturgeon and stuff it with the following: One clove of garlic, two or three sprigs of fennel-top, six cloves, several leaves of marjoram and thyme; tie up the fish with string. Take a saucepan and fry in olive oil some finely chopped celery, thyme, marjoram, and five or six anchovies cleaned and pounded. Put your sturgeon in the saucepan, season with pepper and salt, brown it on both sides and then baste it continually with fish stock or common broth till cooked. Serve it with the above sauce.

TURBOT AU VIN BLANC

UT the turbot in white wine and leave it there for not less than three hours. Take a saucepan and put in it a piece of butter, some chopped herbs such as thyme, marjoram, basil, a clove of garlic; and a pinch of flour. Fry lightly.

Put your turbot in; brown it on both sides, add two ounces of chopped walnuts and the wine in which the fish has been lying. Boil gently till cooked; then serve with lemon slices round it.

TURBOT WITH CHAMPAGNE

AVE some good veal stock in a sauce-pan, into which you will put also your turbot and one onion, some parsley, thyme, two bay-leaves, and four cloves. Season with pepper and salt and put it on the fire. Boil gently for a quarter of an hour; then add half a bottle of white wine and bring the turbot to cook.

When cooked take the fish out and strain the liquid. Put the liquid on the fire again with several sliced mushrooms in it. When these are cooked, place the turbot once more in the saucepan, and when hot serve it with the liquid and mushrooms.

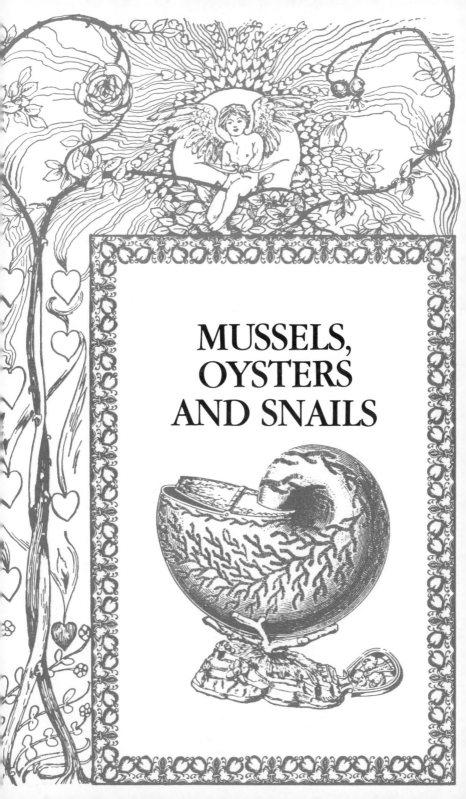

MUSSELS,
OYSTERS
AND SNAILS

TO BROIL OYSTERS

EMOVE from their shells the biggest oysters you can get. Then take a little minced thyme, grated nutmeg, grated bread, and a pinch of salt; season the oysters with this. Have ready their shells cleaned, place them on the gridiron, and put two or three oysters in each shell with a small piece of butter on the top.

Let them cook till the liquor bubbles low. When crisp feed them with a little wine. Sprinkle them with grated nutmeg and serve them.

MUSSELS À LA MARINIÈRE

TAKE four dozen mussels, wash them, brush them and scrub them very well, then put them into a saucepan over a good fire with a little butter, some chopped shallot, parsley and chervil. As soon as the mussels are open, they are done. So lower the fire, pour a glassful of dry white wine over them, stir in a piece of sweet butter, give them a grating of pepper, and serve them almost at once with some freshly chopped parsley sprinkled over them.

A French recipe.

OYSTER COCKTAIL

EASON the oysters with a little chopped shallot, one tablespoon of wine-vinegar, half a tablespoon of tomato sauce, a few drops of Worcester sauce, and a little chopped parsley.

OYSTER OLIVE

RAP each oyster, after shelling it, in a thin slice of lean bacon and fasten them with a wooden toothpick. Put them in a baking-pan and then into the hot oven till the bacon is cooked.

Serve them with chopped parsley sprinkled over them, and a drop of Worcester sauce.

OYSTERS IN FRICASSEE

UT a little butter into a stewpan, a slice of ham, a bundle of sweet herbs, and an onion stuck with two cloves. Stew it a little on a slow fire, then add a little flour, some good broth, and a piece of lemon peel. Then put scalded oysters to it, and simmer them a little. When it is ready, thicken it with the yolks of two eggs, a little cream, and a bit of butter. Take out the ham, bundle of herbs, onion and lemon peel, and squeeze in a lemon.

OYSTERS IN CHAMPAGNE

BOIL in a saucepan a spoonful of fish-glaze, a glass of champagne, and a bunch of assorted herbs.

Open the oysters and drain them on a sieve, collecting the liquid, which you must add to your sauce.

Having reduced the sauce on the fire, plunge the oysters into it, letting them boil for one minute; then serve on toast.

Not everybody cares to treat oysters in this fashion.

OYSTERS IN WINE

 HEAT the oysters in their shells. Open them, take them out and collect their liquid in a pot. Put the oysters in a frying-pan with butter, a sprig of garlic, mint, marjoram, pounded peppercorns, and cinnamon. As soon as they are fried add their liquor and a glass of Malmsey or another generous wine. Serve them on toast.

SNAILS À LA C.C.C. N. I.

EED your snails for a fortnight on milk. This is not difficult; you have only to put the snails in an earthen vessel and cover it with a lid. Every morning just pour a glass of milk on the snails.

When the time for cooking them has arrived, put the snails in an infusion composed of water, vinegar, and salt, and leave them there over-night. In the morning wash them well under the tap and then boil them in water.

After this take them out of their shells, dip them in beaten eggs and fry them in olive oil. Before serving flavour them with elaeologarum, which is a sauce much used by the old Romans, and composed of lovage, coriander, rue, oil, and fish-stock.

My friend C.C.C. knows how to make this sauce to perfection.

SNAILS À LA C.C.C. N. II.

PUT in a stewpan four ounces of butter for fifty snails, and set in on a good fire; when melted, sprinkle in it a teaspoonful of flour, stirring awhile; then add a teaspoonful of parsley chopped fine, two sprigs of thyme, a bay-leaf, a pint of white wine, and then the snails, which you have previously put back into their shells; cover the whole with warm broth, boil gently till the sauce is reduced and the snails are cooked, and serve them mouth upwards, and filled with the sauce.

SNAILS À LA C.C.C. N. III.

BOIL the snails for about twenty minutes in salt water. Then take them out of the shells.

Chop some rosemary, an onion, garlic, and parsley, and put them to fry in olive oil in a saucepan; place the snails in it and season with pepper and salt. After a few minutes add a handful of fresh or dry mushrooms, half a cup of broth, and a little tomato sauce dissolved in water.

Let them boil for about a quarter of an hour and then pour in a glass of strong red wine and let the snails cook.

An old friend ate this dish in Bolgidinga when he was there, and declares that he found himself at least ten years younger.

SNAILS À LA CINQUECENTO

AKE thirty snails ready for cooking. Put them in a pot with red wine and water half and half, a glass of vermouth, a little thyme, two bay-leaves, a clove of garlic, some parsley. Season with pepper and salt.

Boil them in the above for about an hour. Then take them out and shell them, cleaning them of the dark part at the bottom.

Now beat an egg with olive oil in a plate, together with a pinch of salt and pepper, and place your snails in it, leaving them there for a few hours. After this take them out and roll them in bread-crumbs.

Take some silver skewers and fix on each of them eight or nine of the snails. Grill them lightly, and finish cooking in a hot oven.

EGGS

CAVIARE OMELETTE

OUR fresh eggs well beaten, a small spoonful of grated bread, two spoonfuls of caviare, a pinch of chopped chives, one of parsley and a little grated lemon peel. Mix everything together.

Put on the fire a frying-pan with some butter in it and when boiling throw in the above mixture, seeing that you make it cover the bottom of the frying-pan, as one does in making pancakes. When cooked on one side, turn it over in order to cook it on the other side. Serve flat.

EGGS À LA GRUYÈRE

UT some rounds of stale bread. Fry them in butter. Poach the required number of eggs, trim them to the same size as the croûtons, place one on each of these, season with Nepaul or Cayenne pepper, and cover thickly with grated Gruyère cheese. Put a little butter over each egg, and place them on a baking-sheet. Brown them under the grill so as to brown the surface quickly.

EGGS IN MATELOTE

UT a bottle of claret in a stewpan and set it on a good fire; add to it two sprigs of parsley, one of thyme, a clove of garlic, a middling-sized onion, a clove, a bay-leaf, salt and pepper; boil fifteen minutes; then take all the seasonings out and have your wine boiling gently. Break one egg in by letting it fall gently in order to have it entire, then take it out immediately with a skimmer, and place it on a dish; do the same with eight eggs; keep them in a warm (but not hot) place. After which put into the wine, without taking it from the fire, four ounces of butter kneaded with a tablespoonful of flour; boil till reduced to a proper thickness, pour it on the eggs, and serve.

FAISCEDDA (BROAD BEANS TART): A SARDINIAN DISH

NE pound and a half of shelled broad beans. Cook them in water with a pinch of salt. When cooked peel them and pound in the mortar. Mix them with eight fresh eggs, without beating them, three spoonfuls of sugar, one of grated bread, a pinch of grated nutmeg, one of cinnamon.

Work the mixture for a little time and make it into a flat paste of about a finger thick. Put it on the fire in a frying-pan with a little oil already boiling. Fry on both sides till it has a golden crust. Serve hot.

GINESTRATA

IX yolks of egg, which you beat, adding little by little a glass of Madeira, a cupful of cold chicken broth, and a teaspoonful of powdered cinnamon.

Pass through a sieve. Cook in an earthenware pot over a gentle fire. Stir constantly, adding a small piece of butter.

When it gets a little thick, take it out, pour it into cups, serve hot with nutmeg and sugar sprinkled over.

(A Renaissance recipe.)

PIMENTO OMELETTE N. I.

UT into equal small pieces some shallots, stoned black olives, and fillets of anchovies. Fry these lightly in oil. Add three Spanish peppers (pimento), cut into thin strips.

Beat the eggs for the omelette, then incorporate the above ingredients. Put a spoonful of olive oil in a frying-pan. When this boils, pour in the above ingredients and cook it as an ordinary omelette. Serve with tomato sauce.

PIMENTO OMELETTE N. II.

OFTEN in butter or lard some sliced Spanish peppers, add a pinch of Cayenne pepper and mix with the beaten eggs to make an omelette in the usual way.

SCRAMBLED EGGS AND KIDNEY

AKE four kidneys, cut them into thin slices; put them to cook with a small piece of butter and some chopped parsley. After one or two minutes, add a few tomatoes already peeled and cleaned and chopped, pepper and salt. Let the kidneys stew for not more than five minutes, then put in the eggs and scramble them till cooked.

ENTRÉES

ANDOUILLES

AKE some pig's guts. Wash them well, and cut them into pieces about seven inches long. Put them in water with a fourth part of vinegar, some thyme, bay-leaves, a crushed clove of garlic, and keep them there over-night in order to lose the smell of pork.

The next morning take your guts, cut some of them into thin slices; leave the others uncut, in order to fill them in. Cut some fat and some lean meat of pork into thin fillets, mix them together with the sliced guts, add a pinch of salt and pepper, and fill the guts which you have left apart. Be careful to fill them only about a third, otherwise they will burst in cooking. Tie them with string at both ends.

When this is done, put them to boil in an equal mixture of water and milk with a little salt, thyme, bay-leaves and cloves, and also a little fat. Cook them for at least three hours, then let them cool in the liquid in which they have been boiled.

When you want to eat them, take them out and grill them.

This recipe works in the opposite direction, with me. P.B.

71

BRAIN OF BEEF FRIED

CLEAN the brain after having soaked it in hot water, and cut it into eight pieces. Mix well together a little flour, chopped parsley and chives, also a pinch of all-spice; roll the pieces of brain in it, so as to allow the mixture to adhere to them; have some butter in a frying-pan on the fire, and when hot put the pieces of brain in it; fry gently, and serve with fried parsley around.

BRAIN OF VEAL
À LA MUSTAFA

CALD two brains of veal in hot water and clean well. Put them to cook in white wine together with a *bouquet garni* composed of half a clove of garlic, a sprig of rosemary, two cloves, a few leaves of parsley and a small piece of celery.

Have ready some small white onions already boiled, which you add to the brain. When the brains are cooked, take out the *bouquet garni,* slice over the brains some black truffles and serve in the same receptacle in which they have been cooked.

BRAIN WITH TRUFFLES

A CALF'S or two sheeps' brains. Clean them well of red veins. Put the brains into a deep pan over the fire with butter, and when brown on either side place over them a layer of finely sliced truffles. Before serving, sprinkle with grated Parmesan cheese.

CURRIED KIDNEYS

RY In a stewpan a minced shallot till brown in butter, then add a gill of curry sauce and stir over the fire till it boils. Now add a teaspoonful of chopped chutney. Reduce a little and strain. Skin six kidneys and cut them in half, remove the cores and dip them into warm butter, then roll them in flour seasoned with a little curry powder. Melt an ounce of butter in a pan and fry in it the kidneys. Remove them directly they are done, and drain them. Dish up on rounds of hot buttered toast, serve a little of the prepared sauce in the centre of the kidneys. Serve with boiled rice done in the Indian fashion.

GOOSE KIDNEYS

ARTIAL asserts that taking the kidneys of the goose pounded with pine-seeds, sugar, pepper, cinnamon and fresh yolks of eggs, made into croquettes, cooked lightly in the oven, is admirable for warming cold spirits.

KIDNEYS WITH CHAMPAGNE

AKE some kidneys. Cut into thin slices, put in a saucepan over a gently fire with butter, salt and pepper, nutmeg, and sliced mushrooms. When nearly cooked add a pinch of flour and a full glass of champagne. Before serving add a small piece of butter and lemon juice.

LAMBS' EARS
WITH SORREL

ABOUT a dozen of lambs' ears will make a small dish, and these must be stewed. Take a large handful of sorrel, chop it a little and stew it in a spoonful of broth and a morsel of butter. Pour in a small ladle of coulis, grate some nutmeg, and put in a little pepper and salt. Stew it a few minutes, twist up the ears nicely, and dish it up.

MACARONI WITH KIDNEY

A QUARTER of a pound of kidney. A pound of short macaroni (not spaghetti). Chop the kidney fine, put in a deep pan with butter which is already boiling, add a good pinch of spice, cinnamon, pepper, salt, and two or three cloves. To prevent its sticking to the pan, baste it very slowly with drops of old red wine; of this wine use a good glass-full, but pour it over the kidney drop by drop.

Meanwhile the macaroni should be cooked in salted water. It should be well drained. Put it in the above sauce, and mix well. Add a good piece of butter, and cover the macaroni with plenty of grated parmesan cheese. Put in a moderate oven for five minutes and serve.

PIE OF BULLS' TESTICLES

THIS recipe comes out of Scappi's old cookery book.

To make a pie of bulls' testicles, take four of them and boil them in water and salt. Strip them of the membranes that cover them. Cut them in slices, sprinkle them with white pepper, salt, cinnamon and nutmeg.

Prepare apart a mince of lambs' kidney, gravy, three slices of lean ham, a good pinch of chopped marjoram, thyme, and three cloves.

Prepare the pastry for the pie. Then begin to make a layer on your pie dish with the ham, then a layer of slices of testicles, sprinkle well with the mince, and so on. Add, before shutting the pie, a glass of wine. Put it in the oven and serve hot.

SPARROWS' BRAINS

 PARROWS have always been praised as stimulants. Aristotle has written: *Propter nimium coitum, vix tertium annum elabuntur.* Recommended also by the school of Salerno.

Whoever wants to test this should take several brains of male sparrows and half quantity of the brains of pigeons which have not yet begun to fly. Take a turnip and a carrot and boil them in chick-pea broth. Cut in little slices the turnip and carrot, and put them in a deep pan with half a glass of goat's milk, and boil till the milk is almost absorbed. Now put in the brains and sprinkle them with powdered clover seeds. Take off from the fire as soon as they come to the boil, and serve hot.

SWEETBREADS AS HEDGEHOGS

AVING scalded your sweetbreads, lard them with ham and truffles, cut in small pieces. Fry them a short time in butter, and let the pieces stick out a little to make the appearance of bristles. Simmer them in the same butter, with broth and a little white wine, and a very little salt and pepper. When they are done, skim and strain the sauces, add a little coulis, and serve them up.

A European friend writes of this recipe: "Admirable: *Crede experto.*"

SWEETBREADS WITH MUSHROOMS

PARBOIL the sweetbreads and clean them well. Cut them into small pieces and put them into a saucepan with a piece of butter, pepper and salt. Let them *sauter* for five minutes. Add the mushrooms and a few slices of truffles and a cup of broth. Let this stew slowly over a moderate fire for ten minutes.

TESTICLES OF LAMB

AKE some of these testicles, clean them and remove the membranes. Put them in a deep pan with capon fat or a little butter. Cook them slowly on both sides. As soon as they have absorbed the butter or the capon fat, add a good-sized pinch of powdered cinnamon, two or three cloves, and a pinch of saffron. When nearly cooked add the juice of half a lemon.

(From the book of Cartolomeo Scappi, private cook to His Holiness Pope Pius V.)

VEAL SWEETBREADS À LA D'AYEN

BLANCH two veal sweetbreads, and keep only the central part, which you should leave to cool; add half an ounce of bacon, half an ounce of veal fat, and half an ounce of oxtail marrow; salt, pepper, pimento, parsley, garlic, shallots; chop it all up very fine, and mix thoroughly.

In another pan dissolve a yolk of egg in two spoonfuls of milk; pour in the mince of sweetbreads prepared as described; mix it all well together and put into a buttered mould.

Cook in a *bain Marie;* just before serving pour over it several spoonfuls of stock.

Another reliable stimulant.

YELLOW SAUSAGES

OR every ten pounds of chopped lean meat of pork, take one pound of grated cheese, two ounces of pepper, one of cinnamon, one of ginger, one of cloves, one of grated nutmeg, and a good pinch of saffron. Season with salt. Put everything in a mortar and pound well. Now put it in a saucepan with a glass of old white wine and cook over a gentle fire till the wine has been absorbed. Have ready some pig's guts which you have washed first in hot water and afterwards in wine, fill them in with the above, tie them well at both ends, and when you want to eat them, just put them in boiling water for five minutes and serve hot.

Could not be better.

MUSHROOMS
AND
TRUFFLES

BAKED TRUFFLES

 HOOSE some good white truffles; wash with care; wrap each of them in five or six pieces of paper previously soaked in water.

Cook in hot cinders, remove the sheets of paper, dry the truffles, and serve them hot among the folds of a well warmed table-napkin.

Familiar, and yet too little eaten.

FRICASSEE OF MUSHROOMS

AVING peeled your mushrooms, and scraped the inside of them, throw them into cold water. If they are buttons, rub them with flannel; take them out, and boil them in fresh water with salt. When they are tender, put in a little shredded parsley, and an onion stuck with cloves, and toss them up with a good lump of butter rolled in a little flour. You may put in three spoonfuls of thick cream, and a little nutmeg cut in pieces; but be sure to take out the nutmeg and onion before you send it to table.

MUSHROOMS BORDELAISE

AKE some large mushrooms. After having cleaned and skinned them and cut off the stalks, make a small incision on the top. Soak in olive oil, pepper and salt for about two hours. Make apart a hash of garlic, thyme and parsley.

As soon as the mushrooms are taken out of the infusion they should be put on the grill. Cover them with the hash and continue to moisten them with their oil.

Before serving, sprinkle them with a little lemon juice.

PURÉE OF TRUFFLES

AKE some white truffles, clean them well and grate finely. Have a béchamel sauce ready and mix it with the grated truffles, add a glass of sherry and two spoonfuls of cream. Season, and warm up lightly. Avoid bringing it to the boil.

SALAD OF TRUFFLES

 HOP some white truffles and put them in a saucepan on the fire with a glass of sherry for a few minutes. Take the saucepan off the fire and let the truffles cool. When cold, put them in a dish with a spoonful of oil, pepper and salt, teaspoonful of chopped tarragon, and chopped parsley. When you have mixed all together, cover them with mayonnaise sauce.

STEWED MUSHROOMS

LEAN your mushrooms and cut them into thin slices. Chop a little parsley, half a clove of garlic, and some chives. Put them together with the mushrooms with two tablespoons of olive oil in a saucepan, pepper and salt, and let all simmer slowly. If the mushrooms get dry, add a little stock.

TRUFFLES AU GRATIN

CUT some round truffles into two equal parts, and with a sharp spoon scoop a hole in each half.

The middle part that you have scooped out should be cut into small squares, which should be mixed with an equal quantity of foie gras. Salt the mixture, amalgamate with a little brown sauce, and reduce it over heat. Now stuff with this the holes you have scooped out in the middle of the truffles; arrange the halved truffles one beside the other in a deep saucepan containing a little white wine, boil all together, and shut the saucepan in the oven and take it out in a few minutes.

Arrange the truffles on a dish and serve.

POULTRY
AND
GAME

BARON OF HARE

 HOOSE a hare of about eight pounds, cut off the baron and lard it with ham or bacon, and roast it on the spit or in the oven till completely done.

Prepare apart a sauce made with shallots and onions chopped finely, vinegar, and some broth, seasoned with salt and pepper. When these ingredients are cooked, pass everything through a sieve, add the blood of the hare mixed with the liver already pounded in the mortar; re-cook, and pass it through the sieve. Pour this sauce over the roasted baron and serve hot.

Highly recommended, like the following two.

BREAST OF CHICKEN WITH TRUFFLES

REPARE some breasts of chicken, season with pepper and salt. Line a frying-pan with thin slices of ham, put on the top the breasts, sprinkle them with chopped parsley, basil, and a few fennel seeds. Fry them till well coloured.

Arrange them on a fire-proof dish, put on the top a thick layer of sliced white truffles, add a glass of sherry and put it in a hot oven for a few minutes.

CHICKEN AND RICE

UT in quarters a young chicken, season with salt and pepper, and leave them apart. Put on the fire a casserole with a quarter of a pound of chopped ham or bacon. When this is of a golden colour, put on the top two large onions sliced in rings, two sliced carrots, the same amount of celery cut in small pieces, and some sliced mushrooms. On the top of these put half a pound of rice, season with salt and a teaspoonful of paprika, add enough broth or water to cover everything, and place now on the top the chicken. Put the cover on the saucepan and let it simmer slowly for about an hour. Shake the casserole from time to time, but do not stir. Serve hot with grated Parmesan cheese.

CHICKEN BREASTS AND TRUFFLES

 UT the breasts of a roast chicken into small pieces; put them in a casserole with several tablespoonfuls of béchamel sauce, add a piece of butter and a glass of sherry, and reduce the sauce on a hot fire.

Have your truffles clean and sliced, cook them apart in a little butter and a little stock. They must be slightly cooked. Then put them in the middle of a dish and place the strips of chicken breast around them. Serve hot.

CHICKEN GUMBO

UT in very small squares one ounce of raw ham and an onion, put it into a saucepan with a piece of butter, and the wings of a chicken cut into small pieces. When beginning to colour slightly, add three glasses of stock, and a pinch of barley. Boil an hour. Half an hour before serving, put in ten okra-pods cut in slices, five tablespoonfuls of tomato sauce and a little red pepper.

Delicious!

CRANE

LEAN and truss a young crane, and put it in an earthenware saucepan with some water and vinegar, pepper and salt. Let it cook gently. When the liquid is reduced to half, take out the bird and put it in another saucepan with a little olive oil, a bunch of marjoram, some coriander seeds, and some stock. Let it simmer for nearly an hour, then add a glass of red wine which has been boiled previously, with a spoonful of honey, some lovage cummin, benzoin root, and carraway seeds. If necessary add a little starch to thicken the liquid.

When cooked put the bird on a dish, and pour the sauce over it. Wild duck may be treated in the same way.

CURRIED CHICKEN

UT some slices of ham and some onions chopped very fine into a saucepan with a piece of butter; put it on the fire; add a chicken divided in half; cook it rapidly till it colours.

Take the milk of one cocoanut and boil it gently; pour it over your ragout.

Add two tablespoonfuls of curry powder; cook on a slow fire for an hour and three-quarters.

A favourite with elderly epicures.

DUCKS À LA MODE

AKE two ducks, slit them down the backs and bone them carefully. Make a forcemeat of the crumb of a small loaf, four ounces of fat bacon scraped, a little parsley, thyme, lemon-peel, two shallots or onions shred very fine, with pepper, salt, and nutmeg to your taste, and two eggs. Stuff your ducks with this, and sew them up. Then lard them down each side of the breast with bacon, dredge them well with flour, and put them into a Dutch oven to brown. Then put them into a stewpan with three pints of gravy, a glass of red wine, a teaspoonful of lemon-pickle, a large one of walnut and mushroom catchup, one of browning, and an anchovy, with Cayenne pepper to your taste. Stew them gently over a slow fire for an hour; and when they are cooked enough, thicken your gravy, and put in a few truffles and morels. Strain your gravy and pour it upon them.

HARE CROQUETTES

HESE are made with the remains of a roast hare. Take the flesh from the bones and chop it well or pass through the mincing machine; season with pepper, salt, and mixed ground spice, a small chopped onion, the flavour of garlic, and a little ground ginger. Add some grated Parmesan cheese and bread-crumbs. Bind the mixture with eggs. Make it into small croquettes, roll them in grated bread, and fry in hot olive oil or butter.

PAPRIKA CHICKEN

UT a young chicken into joints, fry in butter with one onion cut in rings. When browned remove the chicken, put it in a casserole, and add a cup of good broth and a pinch of salt.

Let it simmer gently for half an hour. Dissolve a dessert-spoonful of paprika in a quarter of a pint of milk in which you put also the same amount of cream, and add it to the chicken. Let it then cook for another half hour.

PARTRIDGES
WITH OLIVES

 LEAN two partridges and brown them in butter in a casserole over a gentle fire; add half a pint of good stock, pepper and salt, two handfuls of stoned black olives and few sliced mushrooms. When nearly cooked, add a Madeira glass of marsala or sherry. Serve in the casserole.

PHEASANT
À LA HANNIBAL

HOOSE a not too tender pheasant, put it in an earthenware pot with a veal marrow bone. Add water to cover it up to three fingers, and put also a whole piece of cinnamon, some pieces of dried apricots, prunes, cherries, pine-nuts, saffron, cloves, and some chopped mushrooms. Boil with the cover well sealed, but before covering it add a glass of white wine, a little vinegar and sugar, and cook.

Simply delicious!

PISH-PASH

CUT up a raw chicken into small joints. Have ready one onion, one shallot, a few cloves, five or six peppercorns, a bay-leaf, and a sprig of thyme. Put the chicken and ingredients into a stewpan with enough cream to cover it. Salt it, and let it simmer for about an hour. Take up the chicken, strain the liquor and then put it back with the chicken into the pan, and add two or three ounces of rice. When the rice is well cooked, serve hot.

POTTED PIGEONS

RAW and clean. Break the legs just above the feet; leave enough below the joint to tie down to the tail. Wash and wipe. If old and tough, cover them with vinegar, spiced and flavoured with onion, and let them stand several hours. This makes them tender. Drain and wipe. Dredge with salt, pepper, and flour.

Fry several slices of salt pork; cut one large onion fine, and fry in the salt pork fat. Put the crisp fat in the stewpan, add the fried onion, then brown the pigeons all over in the fat left in the pan. Put them in the stewpan; add boiling stock enough to half cover them; add a pinch of herbs tied in a bag. Simmer from one to three hours, or till the pigeons are tender. Remove the fat from the broth, season to taste, and thicken with flour and butter cooked together. Strain over the pigeons, and serve hot.

QUAILS À LA LUCULLUS

CLEAN well six quails.

Cut three or four ounces of ham into small pieces, chop one shallot, put both ham and shallot in a saucepan with a little butter and fry; then add eight chicken livers, a small *bouquet garni,* six peppercorns, two cloves, pepper and salt. Let this all cook gently; when cooked, pound in the mortar, pass through a sieve, then add some sliced truffles.

With this stuff the quails, oil them with the best olive oil, wrap them in greased paper, and cook them in the oven.

QUAILS WITH TRUFFLES

RUSS the quails and cook them on a slow fire for half an hour on a foundation composed of chopped bacon and two sliced carrots, two sliced onions, a branch of celery chopped fine, a pinch of thyme and one small bayleaf. Pour over the quails when in the saucepan a glass of sherry. Take out your quails, put them in a "cocotte", have the liquor strained, and pour it over the quails. Reduce the liquid on the fire. When nearly cooked make a layer, on the top, of sliced black truffles, and serve in the "cocotte".

RÔTI SANS PAREIL

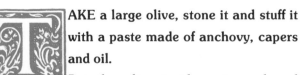

AKE a large olive, stone it and stuff it with a paste made of anchovy, capers and oil.

Put the olive inside a trussed and boned bec-figue (garden warbler).

Put the bec-figue inside a fat ortolan.

Put the ortolan inside a boned lark.

Put the stuffed lark inside a boned thrush.

Put the thrush inside a fat quail.

Put the quail, wrapped in vine-leaves, inside a boned lapwing.

Put the lapwing inside a boned golden plover.

Put the plover inside a fat, boned, red-legged partridge.

Put the partridge inside a young, boned, and well-hung woodcock.

Put the woodcock, rolled in bread-crumbs, inside a boned teal.

Put the teal inside a boned guinea-fowl.

Put the guinea-foul, well larded, inside a young and boned tame duck.

Put the duck inside a boned and fat fowl.

Put the fowl inside a well-hung pheasant.

Put the pheasant inside a boned and fat wild goose.

Put the goose inside a fine turkey.

Put the turkey inside a boned bustard.

Having arranged your roast after this fashion, place it in a saucepan of proper size with onions stuffed with cloves, carrots, small squares of ham, celery, mignonette, several strips of bacon well seasoned, pepper, salt, spice, coriander seeds, and two cloves of garlic.

Seal the saucepan hermetically by closing it with pastry. Then put it for ten hours over a gentle fire, and arrange it so that the heat penetrates evenly. An oven moderately heated would suit better than the hearth.

Before serving, remove the pastry, put your roast on a hot dish after having removed the grease, if there is any, and serve.

———

(Abbreviated from *Le Parfait Cuisinier* of A. T. Raimbault, 1814.)

It might be difficult to procure so varied an assortment of wild fowls anywhere at one and the same time; difficult, too, to find bustards anywhere nowadays; difficult, too, to stuff a bigger bird like the lapwing into a smaller one like the plover. I observe with sorrow that the common partridge, one of the best of all game birds, is not represented in this aviary.

STEWED TURKEY

UT in a large stew-kettle half a pound of bacon cut in slices, four ounces of knuckle of veal, three sprigs of parsley, two of thyme, a bay-leaf, six small onions, one carrot cut in four pieces, three cloves, one clove of garlic, salt, pepper, and then the turkey; wet with a pint of white wine, same of broth, cover as nearly air-tight as you can, place in a moderately-heated oven or on a moderate fire, let simmer (not boil) about two hours and a half, then turn it over, put back on the fire or in the oven for another two hours and a half, after which dish the turkey; strain the sauce and put it back on the fire to reduce it to a jelly, which you spread on it, and serve.

STUFFED CAPON

HE capon must be young and tender. When trussed and cleaned, stuff it with the following ingredients: minced meat of veal, ham cut into small squares, chopped aromatic herbs, some foie-gras, a few slices of white truffles, pepper and salt.

Put the stuffed capon in a saucepan after having covered the bottom with some bacon and rings of onions. Pour over the capon a glass of white wine, reduce on the fire till well thickened, then add one cup of broth and let it simmer gently for an hour and a half.

Dish the capon and pour the sauce over it, after having passed it through a sieve.

TURKEY IN
THE ITALIAN WAY

HAVING minced the liver of a young turkey very fine with some chopped parsley and some fresh mushrooms, some pepper, salt, and more than an ounce of butter, mix them well together, and put them into the body of the turkey. Put a piece of butter into a stewpan, some shallots, and pepper and salt. When it is hot, put in the turkey, turn it often, that it may be of a fine brown, and lay it to cool. Then lay over it some slices of bacon, and cover it all over with paper; put it upon a spit, and lay it down to roast.

In the meantime, cut some large mushrooms fine, with a good quantity of parsley, and a few green onions cut small. Pour half a pint of white wine into a saucepan, and, as soon as it is hot, put in these ingredients; add some pepper and salt, the juice of a lemon, and cloves of garlic. Let them boil, and then put in a quarter of a pint of rich gravy, and a small teacupful of oil. Let all boil up once or twice, then take out the garlic, and put in a piece of butter rolled in flour. Lay the turkey in the dish, and pour the sauce over it.

Much ado about nothing.

TURKEY WITH PICKLED PORK AND ONIONS

AKE twenty-four small white onions and boil them in broth, with half a pound of pickled pork cut into thin slices, a bundle of parsley, some green shallots, some thyme, two cloves, and a little whole pepper and salt. As soon as they be done, drain them, put them into the turkey, and wrap it in slices of bacon, and paper over it, and then roast it.

Make a sauce with a piece of butter, a slice of ham, two shallots, and a few mushrooms. Let them soak a little, and then add two spoonfuls of broth, and as much coulis. Simmer it about an hour, skim it, and drain it. When the whole is ready, add a small spoonful of mustard, a little pepper and salt, and serve it up.

Jews of a certain age could profit by this, if it were not for the pork.

MEAT

ARISTA

HIS is a pretentious name for roast pork, but its derivation, if correct, is interesting. In 1430 the Greek and Roman Bishops held a Council in Florence to discuss some question concerning the Roman and Greek Churches. One day at dinner they were served with this roast pork, which the Greek Bishops liked so much that they cried "Arista" (excellent!). Since then roast pork flavoured with rosemary and garlic is Arista for the Florentines, and roast pork for everybody else. Here is the recipe:

Clean your loin of pork of the skin the part of the fat; make little holes in the meat and in each hole put pepper, salt, a clove of garlic, a spray of rosemary, and a clove or two. Salt well outside and put it to roast on the spit or in the oven. When cooked you may call it Arista, if you like.

BREAST OF MUTTON IN CASSEROLE

EMOVE all the outer skin of the breast of mutton and wash it well. Chop finely two shallots, some parsley, four leaves of basil or thyme, three boned anchovies, and the meat of three or four sausages, or more if the breast is a big piece. Mix well together, adding a pinch of pepper and salt, and with this stuff the breast of mutton. Roll it and tie it with string.

Put it on the fire in a casserole together with a glass of white wine and half a cup of good stock; season with salt. When the meat is nearly cooked, skim the liquor well, and add a piece of butter as big as a walnut, previously rolled in flour. When ready put the joint on a hot dish and pour its sauce over it.

BREAST OF VEAL AU BASILIC

 UT the meat into small pieces and put it for a few minutes in boiling water. Then cook it in a saucepan with a small piece of butter, a cup of good broth, together with some parsley, a bay-leaf, a clove of garlic, a little thyme, two cloves, and several leaves of fresh basil, pepper and salt. Let it simmer till the meat has absorbed all the liquor and till the above herbs and garlic have practically got into a pulp and are attached to the meat. Then take the pieces of veal out of the saucepan one by one, and put them to cool on a dish. When cold dip them into beaten eggs and roll them into grated bread. Fry them in butter and serve hot with slices of lemon round them.

CHILO

AKE some chops from a neck of mutton, put them in a stewpan with a small piece of butter and brown them, season with pepper and salt. Add some fresh peas, four or five small onions, about a dozen cloves and cover with light stock or water.

Cook gently till the mutton is tender and serve in its stewpan.

CUTLETS OF VEAL EN PAPILLOTES

UT the cutlets thin, season with pepper and salt, and sprinkle with chopped parsley and grated cheese; on the top put several slices of mushrooms and onions cut in rings, and a piece of butter. Wrap up each cutlet in a piece of buttered paper, put them on a fire-proof dish and cook them in the oven. Serve hot in their papillotes.

CUTLETS OF WILD BOAR

AKE away the fat around the cutlets and put them in an infusion of rose-vinegar, chopped basil, mint, marjoram, and the juice of a lemon. Leave in this infusion over-night.

When you take them out, dry them with a cloth and stick in each cutlet two or three cloves, season with pepper and salt, and grill them over a bright fire.

When cooked, sprinkle the cutlets with cinnamon powder, put them on a hot dish, garnish with sliced oranges, and serve with caper sauce.

FALSU MAGRU

AKE enough lean of beef to make ten thin slices, which you beat well. Season them with pepper and salt. Spray on the top of each one a little layer of butter, sprinkle over some grated cheese mixed with grated bread, some parsley, chillies and sage all finely chopped. Make a layer on the top with sliced boiled eggs, and cover each piece of meat with a slice of ham as big as the meat.

Roll each piece of meat up and tie with string.

Now make the following sauce in a casserole. One onion, one carrot, a piece of celery, two cloves, all finely chopped. Fry these ingredients in the casserole with a piece of butter; when the onion is brown, put in the casserole two cupfuls of broth, with a teaspoonful of tomato sauce. Let this simmer for ten minutes, then add your meat rolls, and let them cook gently till tender. Serve with the sauce over them.

A FLORENTINE OF VEAL

 INCE two kidneys of veal, fat and all, very fine. Chop a few herbs and put them with it, and add some currants. Season them with cloves, mace, nutmeg, and a little salt; four or five yolks of eggs chopped fine, and some crumbs of bread; an apple or two chopped, some candied lemon-peel cut small, a little sherry, and orange-flower water.

Lay a sheet of puff paste at the bottom of your dish, put in the ingredients, and cover it with another sheet of puff paste. Bake it in a gentle oven, and serve up hot, with sugar scraped on the top of it.

LOIN OF BEEF

 AKE a good piece of tender loin. Beat it well, sprinkle it with salt, pepper, cinnamon, powdered ginger, nutmeg, and fennel seeds. Put it in an earthenware pot and cover it with Malmsey wine, and leave it for six hours. When taken out of the infusion it should be covered with strips of bacon tied round it, putting between the bacon and the loin a few cloves. Roast on the spit, basting it with the infusion.

MUTTON CUTLETS WITH COGNAC

AKE some fairly thick cutlets of mutton and lard them with strips of bacon and fillets of anchovy, season with pepper and salt.

Put them in a saucepan with a piece of butter, four medium-sized onions, a little bunch of parsley, half a bay-leaf, a little basil, two cloves and a dozen coriander seeds. After having lightly cooked the cutlets add two tablespoonfuls of good cognac and let them simmer for twenty minutes. Then put the cutlets on a hot dish and strain the liquid over them.

PORK CHOPS WITH FENNEL SEEDS

RY pork chops in their own grease, season with pepper and salt. When fried add two or three pinches of fennel seeds and a spoonful of tomato sauce diluted in hot water. Now let the chops simmer till they have absorbed more than half of the liquid. Take up the chops from the pan, put them on a hot dish and strain over them the liquor. Serve hot.

A stimulant for sturdy stomachs.

PORK IN MILK

AKE a piece of loin of pork. Put to boil apart about a pint of milk with six cloves, a clove of garlic, and a few leaves of sage.

Brown the pork in a pan, drain the fat, and add the milk gradually after having passed it through a strainer. Now let the pork simmer gently till cooked.

A good restorative!

SPICED BEEF

FOUR to six pounds from the middle cut of the shin. Wash the meat on the outside, and cut off any part of the skin which is not sweet and clean. Pick off all the fine fragments of bone. Cut the meat into several pieces; cover with boiling water. Skim carefully as it boils, and then simmer until the meat falls to pieces, and the liquor is reduced to half a pint. Remove the meat; season the liquor highly with salt, pepper, sage, and thyme. Add it to the meat and mix with a fork till the meat is all broken. Pack in a brickloaf pan. When cold, cut in thin slices.

STEWED VENISON

AKE the breast of venison, about three pounds, cut it into pieces, put it in a casserole with half a pound of ham or bacon, pepper and salt, and let it cook for twenty minutes.

Add now *bouquet garni,* half a pint of water and half of white wine. Let it simmer gently; when the meat is nearly cooked, see that the liquor is not too thin; if it is, thicken it with a little flour, which you dissolve in a spoonful of the same liquor. Add then about eight or nine small tomatoes. When the tomatoes are cooked, serve hot in its casserole.

STUFFED PIG'S HEAD

I N France it used to be called Fromage de Cochon. Take a young pig's head already well cleaned. Unbone it as far as possible. Take out all the meat without cutting the skin. Separate the lean from the fat.

Chop finely the lean part and also some of the fat. Cut the ears into long slices, then season this with salt and pepper, some chopped thyme, six cloves, two cloves of garlic, and half a grated nutmeg. With this make layers inside the head-skin; on each layer put a slice of ham and leaves of parsley not chopped, well arranged. Go on till the head-skin is filled. Stitch it with strong string. Wrap it in a cloth, and put to cook in water, with two glasses of white wine, thyme, bay-leaves, two cloves of garlic, two onions, pepper and salt. Let it boil at least six to seven hours. When cooked drain it well and serve cold.

SUCKING-PIG WITH EELS

AKE a sucking-pig ten or fifteen days old, clean it and empty its intestines and all the insides. Stuff these with thick pieces of eel, which have previously been boned and washed with vinegar. Add as stuffing peppercorns, cloves and plenty of sage. This is an extremely appetising and stimulating dish. The eel goes very well with pork, because it is among fish what the pig is among quadrupeds.

VEAL CUTLETS MARMOTTE

AKE some veal cutlets, beat them well, and lard them with small pieces of ham and little bits of anchovy. Put them in a saucepan with a little butter, a *bouquet garni* made of parsley, thyme, two cloves, a piece of fennel and a clove of garlic. On the top of the cutlets put four or five big onions. Pepper and salt. Add half a cup of broth and half a glass of sherry. Let them cook slowly till the onions are tender. Then remove the *bouquet garni* and serve the cutlets with the onions.

I have not tried this dish. Sounds rather dull.

VULVAE STERILES

APICIUS gives five or six recipes for this dish in the VIIth Book, called *Polyteles*. The Romans were very fond of it. Horace praises it in the XVth Epistle, so does Pliny in his Natural History, and Martial too. Here is one recipe, not from Apicius.

Take that part of a sow, clean it well and put it to marinate in white wine, in which you have cooked before a chopped onion, a branch of celery, a pinch of fennel seeds, peppercorns, some ginger, a pinch of saffron, and salt.

After having kept the meat in this infusion for a few hours, take it out and sprinkle it with flour, put it in a casserole over the fire with a small spoonful of olive oil, let it brown on both sides. Strain the infusion, and with it moisten the meat from time to time. When nearly cooked add the juice of a lemon or an orange, and serve hot.

WILD BOAR

THIS animal always needs a complicated way of cooking (and well worth the trouble).

Trim a saddle of boar after having beaten it well. Wash it in vinegar and dry with a cloth. Now pound in a mortar the following: half an ounce of cinnamon, half an ounce of cloves, quarter of an ounce of coriander seeds, the same of fennel seeds and as much of ginger, a pinch of nutmeg and a generous pinch of pepper. Mix all together and sprinkle over the saddle. Now take an earthenware saucepan, put at the bottom some goose fat; if this is impossible to find, butter will do. Lay your wild boar on it, cover it with slices of ham or bacon, add a glass of white wine, and some juniper berries. Put the lid on and seal it with a paste around the rim. Put the saucepan in the oven and leave it for at least three hours without moving it. Serve hot.

VEGETABLES
AND
SALADS

ARTICHOKE BOTTOMS

AVING boiled and drained six artichoke bottoms of a fair size, and scooped out their chokes, give them a dust of salt and pepper and place them in a pan with enough olive oil to save them from burning. Add some aromatic herbs, two cloves of garlic, and put the pan in the oven to bake. When the artichokes are tender, remove the garlic, and before serving squeeze a lemon over them.

Appetising, even if not efficacious.

ARTICHOKES WITH EGGS

EMOVE the outside leaves of six young artichokes. Cut away the top and cut each artichoke in half. Put them in fresh water and leave them there for an hour at least.

Dry them now with a cloth, squeeze between the leaves some drops of lemon juice, and put in a little pepper and salt. Put them on a pan with butter and a pinch of spice and fry over the fire on both sides. Have ready three beaten eggs, pour them over the artichokes, and when the eggs are cooked, serve.

CELERY À LA POPOFF

UT your celery into pieces about a finger long. Put them in a saucepan with a little butter; season with salt, pepper, and nutmeg, and cover it with good stock. Let it simmer till cooked and till the liquor has been nearly absorbed. Put it on a dish, sprinkle with grated cheese and serve hot.

CELERY À LA RAJA

AKE one or two bunches of celery and use only the white part. Cut it into pieces and wash. Now boil the celery for about a quarter of an hour, then take it out of the water and let it cool.

Chop finely an onion, a carrot, some parsley, basil, and marjoram, and fry these ingredients in butter. When fried put the celery on the top, the pepper and salt and a pinch of nutmeg, a cup of good stock, and let it simmer gently for half an hour.

Have ready some slices of sweetbread of veal which you have previously boiled and cleaned, make a layer with them on the top of the celery, add half a glass of Marsala or sherry, and let them all cook slowly.

GIANT PEPPERS (CAPSICUMS) STUFFED

 HESE peppers are good when green or yellow. Free them of the seeds. Put them on the fire on a grill and let them toast a little till you can peel off the skin.

Have ready the following stuffing for each pepper: a slice of ham or bacon, one small veal kidney, a spoonful of Parmesan cheese, some bread-crumbs soaked already in broth, a pinch of parsley, and a quarter of a clove of garlic; chop all this very fine and mix it with sausage meat; season with salt and a small pinch of nutmeg.

Stuff them with this, and then put them in a pan with a little olive oil and cook in a hot oven, moistening them from time to time with broth, in which a spoonful of tomato sauce has been previously dissolved. Serve with the sauce.

PURÉE OF ARTICHOKE BOTTOMS

AKE some artichoke bottoms, with all the leaves off. Scald them to remove any trace of the "choke"; put them in water in which you have mixed a little flour with salt and lemon juice.

When they are cooked, reduce them to pulp, mix them in a béchamel sauce, pass through a sieve, and heat again in butter and cream.

SALAD ROCKET

Nec minus erucas jubeo vitare salaces.
—OVID

Et Veneres revocans eruca morantem.
—MARTIAL

HE who would follow Ovid and Martial should take: twenty leaves of salad rocket, wash them thoroughly, and with half a lettuce and a clove of chopped garlic make into salad, seasoned with salt, pepper, olive oil, and vinegar. Salad rocket is certainly a stimulant.

Recommended by Columella, and by Turner and Culpepper.

STEWED CELERY

UT the celery into pieces a finger long, wash them and boil them in water. When nearly tender take them out, drain, and put them in a saucepan with a piece of butter over a gentle fire. Season with pepper, salt, and spice, and let them simmer for ten minutes. Add a pinch of chopped marjoram, a small piece of butter already rolled in flour, and a cup of fish stock. Cook till the stock has nearly been absorbed.

SAUCES
AND
SAVOURIES

ANCHOVY TOAST

UT some slices of bread, toast nicely, trim to any shape required. Have ready a hot-water plate, on which put four ounces of butter; let it melt; add the yolks of four raw eggs, one tablespoonful of anchovy sauce, Nepaul pepper to taste. Mix all well together, and dip the toast in, both sides; let it well soak into the mixture. Serve very hot, piled on a dish, and garnished with parsley.

Anchovies have long been famed for their lust-provoking virtues.

HORSE-RADISH SAUCE

IX well together: two gills of cream with the same amount of mayonnaise sauce, three spoonfuls of grated horse-raddish, two of vinegar, a pinch of sugar; add a little mustard and serve.

INDIAN SAVOURY

FOUR ounces of Parmesan grated, two ounces of flour, a little butter, one salt-spoon of mustard, a little salt and Nepaul pepper; mix with a well-beaten egg or two, so that the mixture is like a paste; put it in the oven for a minute or two, and then lay it on nicely-cut pieces of toast; put it in the oven again for a minute, and brown the top over with a salamander. Garnish with parsley.

MARROW OF LEOPARD

 TIMID person is advised to sustain himself with the following:

Take a good quantity of leopard's marrow, cook it in goat's milk and abundant white pepper, and eat it on toast.

Medulla pardi bibita mirabilis est.

PONTIFF SAUCE

UT two or three slices of lean veal, and the same of ham, and a small piece of butter, into a stewpan, with some sliced onions, carrots, parsley, and a head of celery. When it is brown, add a little white wine, some good broth, a clove of garlic, four shallots, two cloves, and two slices of lemon peel. Boil it over a slow fire till the juices are extracted from the meat; then skim it, and strain it through a sieve. Just before you use it, add a little coulis, with some parsley chopped very fine.

Try it with macaroni.

RED PEPPERS SAUCE

PUT in a saucepan eight or nine tomatoes together with four red peppers, one onion, one clove of garlic, a spray of rosemary, a pinch of salt.

Let boil gently till the tomatoes are getting thick; add then two glasses of vinegar, a few cloves, a pinch of cinnamon, and let it boil for ten minutes.

Take it out from the fire and let it stand till cold, strain it and keep it in a corked bottle. Can be used cold or hot when needed, for example, with boiled beef or fried eggs.

SHRIMPS AND RICE ON TOAST

OOK your rice in broth and drain it well. Mix it with some chopped shrimps, already boiled, season with salt and put the above on pieces of toast.

Place a small piece of butter on the top and cook for a few minutes in the oven. Serve with Cayenne.

SICILIAN SAUCE

RUISE half a spoonful of coriander seeds, and four cloves, in mortar. Put three-quarters of a pint of good gravy, and a quarter of a pint of essence of ham, into a stewpan. Peel half a lemon, and cut it into very thin slices, and put it in with the coriander seeds and cloves. Let them boil up, and then add three cloves of garlic whole, a head of celery sliced, two bay-leaves, and a little basil. Let these boil till the liquid is reduced to half the quantity. Then put in a glass of white wine, strain it off, and if not thick enough, put in a piece of butter rolled in flour.

This is a good sauce for roast fowls.

TONGUE SAVOURY

AKE a piece of boiled smoked tongue. Pound it in the mortar together with a piece or two of preserved ginger and a few leaves of sage; flavour with French mustard. Coat with this paste some slices of toast and serve.

WINE SAUCE
FOR GAME

HOP an onion and a shallot and fry in butter, when coloured add a crushed clove of garlic, a teaspoonful of chutney, a cupful of broth, a teaspoonful of curry powder, a claret-glass of sherry, a pinch of salt, one of grated nutmeg, a little chopped chilli, and boil for twenty minutes.

Pass through a sieve and dissolve in it two large spoonfuls of currant jelly.

SWEETS

FRITTERS OF ELDER-FLOWER

AKE some elder-flowers and pound them in the mortar, mix them with cream cheese and grated Parmesan, fresh eggs, a pinch of cinnamon, a few drops of rose water. Work the lot into a paste and then form little round cakes or balls.

Fry in butter, serve hot with sugar sprinkled on the top.

(Popular in the *seventeenth* century, and not so bad as it sounds.)

MARMALADE OF CARNATIONS

ALF a pound of sugar, a cup of water and half a pound of fresh red carnations. Crush in a mortar the tops of the carnations, seeing that you use only the red part.

Put the sugar and water in a saucepan and boil to a syrup, add the crushed carnation and boil very slowly till they are in a pulp.

Stir well and pour into little cups.

This compôte is very useful for people of cold temperament.

PISTACHIO CREAM

AKE out the kernels of half a pound of pistachio nuts, beat them in a mortar with a spoonful of brandy, and put them into a tossing-pan, with a pint of cream, and the yolks of two eggs finely beaten. Stir it gently over a slow fire till it is thick, but do not let it boil. Put it into a soup-plate, and when it is cold, stick some kernels, cut long-ways, all over it.

QUINCE JELLY

AKE six or more quinces. Peel them and cut them in slices, put them in a saucepan with half a pound of raisins, half a pound of dry prunes, and half a pound of syruped cherries. Add three glasses of white wine, two of red wine, peppercorns, cloves, a little powdered red ginger, and a handful of pine-nuts. Toast a pound of bread and add this also.

Put all in a saucepan and boil it slowly, stirring continually so that it does not stick to the pan. When cooked, which you will see from the colour and from the quinces having got into a pulp, put it in a mould and let it set.

Mattioli says that if women ate plenty of quinces they would have sons of marked ability and energy.

DRINKS

AN AFTER-LOVE DRINK

NTO a Madeira glass pour: a quarter glass of maraschino, a yolk of egg, a quarter glass of cream, a quarter glass of old brandy. Serve without mixing, seeing that the yolk of egg is not broken. The whole should be swallowed in one gulp.

Highly recommended by my friend Baron de M....

AN APHRODISIAC DRINK

UT together in a glass: two lumps of sugar and eight drops of Curaçao. Fill up the glass with port. Put it in a receptacle and boil it. When just boiling take it off the fire and serve hot with a slice of lemon and nutmeg sprinkled over it.

CINNAMON LIQUEUR

AKE one quart of spirits of wine, twenty drops of oil of cinnamon, two drops of oil of roses, the same of oil of nutmeg. Add one quart of syrup. Filter and put it in bottles.

Cinnamon was famed as an aphrodisiac several centuries ago.

EARLY BIRDS

HEAT a quart of ale mixed with a table-spoonful of powdered ginger and nutmeg. Whisk up three fresh eggs with a gill of cold ale and two ounces of moist sugar. When well frothed up, add the warm ale, by degrees, and a glass of eau-de-vie. When this is done, drink immediately.

GENTIAN WINE

RATE thirty grammes of gentian roots, and leave them to soak for twenty-four hours in two quarts of Fine-champagne. Add a quart of old red wine; cork the bottle and expose it to the sun for eight days; then filter it. It has been found a satisfactory stimulant.

HIPPOGRAS APHRODISIAC

ERE is the recipe for this unrivalled stimulant:

Crushed cinnamon	30 grammes
Ginger	30 "
Cloves	8 "
Vanilla	8 "
White sugar	2 pounds
Red Bourgogne wine	1 quart

HONEY-WINE
(OINOMELI)

AKE some finest fermented grape juice; it will be ready in twenty days after it has been distilled in the vat.

Blanch some honey, stirring vigorously; to one part of it add five of the grape juice, and stir the mixture with a stick. Stir it like this daily for fifty consecutive days, keeping the vessel covered with a cloth, which will let the fume of fermentation escape.

At the end of this time, take off carefully all that is floating on the surface, and shut up the oinomeli in earthenware jars, where you will leave it to mature.

HYDROMEL

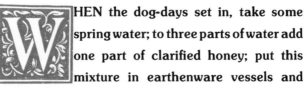

HEN the dog-days set in, take some spring water; to three parts of water add one part of clarified honey; put this mixture in earthenware vessels and have it stirred by your slaves for a long time. Leave it out in the open, covered with a cloth, for forty days and forty nights.

HYSTERICAL WATER

AKE seeds of wild parsnip, betony, and roots of lovage, of each two ounces; roots of single peony four ounces; of mistletoe of the oak three ounces; myrrh a quarter of an ounce, and castor half an ounce. Beat all these together, and add to them a quarter of a pound of dried millepedes. Pour on these three quarts of mugwort water, and two quarts of brandy. Let them stand in a closed vessel eight days, and then still it in a cold still pasted up. You may draw off nine pints of water, and sweeten it to your taste. Mix all together, and bottle it up.

LOVAGE

NE gallon of gin, mixed with one pint clear syrup; add a tincture made by macerating one pound of fresh-cut celery roots and one ounce of fennel in pure spirit for two days. Strain by pressure; add one drachm of oil of cinnamon, thirty drops of oil of carraway seeds, and filter.

LOVING CUP

UT in a bowl some toasted bread; add six ounces of sugar, one lump of sugar saturated in orange-flower essence; grate half a nutmeg and mix it with the same quantity of cinnamon and ginger in powder. Put this in the bowl together with a quart of good ale, one bottle of sherry, and a little soda-water.

The soda-water is the least important of these ingredients, and can be dispensed with.

SORBET OF CHAMPAGNE

N three-quarters of a quart of syrup soak the skins of an orange and of half a lemon; add half a bottle of champagne or Anjou wine, the juice of four oranges and of one lemon, mix it all, pass it through a sieve and freeze it on the ice-freezer. Ten minutes before serving add another half-bottle of wine.

TONIC WINE

N a quart of white wine soak for two days five grammes of juniper berries, fifteen grammes of Calisaia (a kind of Peruvian bark), and fifteen of bitter quassia. Filter the liquid, and mix with an equal quantity of bitter orange syrup. Drink a Madeira glass of this every day.

(Warmly recommended by an aged friend.)

Norman Douglas
1868 — 1932
Fui non sum
Estis non eritis

Pino Orioli
1884 — 1952
Fui non sono
Siete non sarete

These "Epitaphs" on himself and his friend,
G. Orioli, are in Norman Douglas's handwriting and
done on an odd piece of paper at a restaurant in
Florence exactly twenty years before he died. Orioli
died in Lisbon in 1942.

NORMAN DOUGLAS *and* **G. ORIOLI**
on a walking tour in the Vorarlberg

INDEX